THE FREEDOM FIGHTERS WHO PREVENTED THE BTR AND ASSAM (UNDIVIDED GOALPARA AND KAMRUP DISTRICTS) FROM BECOMING A PART OF EAST PAKISTAN (NOW BANGLADESH)

RITURAJ BASUMATARY

Made with ❤ on the Notion Press Platform
www.notionpress.com

Contents

I

Introduction

The deteriorating political and law and order situation in Assam and involvement of political leaders in dividing the society for their personal or party's interest has compelled the citizens to remember the leaders, who saved Assam becoming a part of Pakistan on the eve of India's attaining independence in the year 1947. That was a time when British government conspired to divide the country on religious community basis by creating Hindu and Muslim majority states and leave them quarreling for ever. The present turmoil in the state calls for emergence of a leader like Gopi Nath Bardoloi and other tribal leaders who played a vital role in saving Assam becoming a part of Pakistan more than seven and half decades ago. Had the British Cabinet Mission succeeded in its plan, the history of Assam would have been different one.

The Labour Party government in Britain sent the Mission to explore the possibility of drafting a future Constitution for India in consultation with the Viceroy and the Indian political leaders. The Mission reached India on March 23, 1946 and began discussions with Indian leaders. According to its plan the Union of India would consist of both British India and the Indian states. It arbitrarily divided British India into three groups viz A, B and C. While six Hindu majority provinces of Madras, Bombay, Bihar, Orissa, Central Province and United Province of Agra and Awadh formed group A, Punjab, Sindh, Baluchistan and North West Frontier Provinces in group B. Assam and Bengal were clubbed together in group C. The Cabinet Mission had thorough discussions with the Congress and Muslim League leaders before announcing their plan.

On April 1, 1946 Gopi Nath Bardoloi had an interview with the Mission. He strongly protested inclusion of Assam into group C. He argued Assam was already a province formed on linguistic and cultural basis enjoying provincial autonomy. It should be allowed to continue in the future set-up also as a full-fledged unit, he pleaded. He favoured even separation of Sylhet district from Assam and rejected Mohammed Ali Jinna's demand for Pakistan as absolutely preposterous. The Cabinet Mission stuck to its plan of forming groups.

The Mission's proposal to group Assam with Bengal for creating a predominantly Muslim zone in Eastern India like one proposed to be setup in western India was strongly resented by the people of Assam. According to this plan the Assam representatives to the Constituent Assembly would have to sit in a section with the Bengal representatives to determine the provincial constitution and also a constitution for group C by a simple majority of votes. Except Muslim League, all quarters in Assam protested against this grouping scheme. The Cabinet Mission's announcement of the proposal came out on May 16, 1946. Assam Provincial Congress Committee then in session at Guwahati lodged an emphatic protest with the Congress Working

Committee against it. The Asom Jatiya Mahasabha did some secret papers showing the designs of Muslim League in Assam. There began a feverish agitation in Assam to quash the group scheme, which was but the thin end to be driven into the heart of Assam.

On July 16, 1946 the Assam Legislative Assembly adopted a resolution moved by the Chief Minister (erstwhile premier) Gopinath Bardoloi himself expressing strong disapproval of the plan and directing ten representatives of Assam to the Constituent Assembly elected by the Provincial Assembly not to sit in section with any other province for devising the Constitution of Assam or any group constitution with such other province for settlement of any question relating to Assam.

The discontent in Assam was based on genuine fears. It was clear once Assam was grouped with Muslim majority Bengal to serve the interest of Muslim community her fate would be sealed. Assam would lose her identity and individuality in the political whirlpool of Muslim India, although Assam was not and had never been a Muslim majority province. Gopinath Bardoloi, who became the chief minister of Assam for the second time in February 1946 and continued to lead his ministry through Independence until his death on August 5, 1950 took best opportunity to express his views on the future Constitution of India and the state of Assam within it when the Cabinet Mission invited him for this purpose in April 1946.

The Congress Working Committee took time in giving a clear and bold lead to Assam on this vital issue. On behalf of Gopinath Bardoloi, Bijoy Chandra Bhagawati and Mahendra Mohan Choudhury called on Gandhiji at Srirampur and placed Assam's case before him seeking his advice and guidance at the critical juncture. Strengthened with blessings of Gandhiji, Gopi Nath Bardoloi succeeded at last in convincing the Indian leaders about the Assam's just case and getting this part of the Cabinet Mission's plan scrapped. Had not Assam opposed the grouping scheme, the formal establishment of Pakistan might have been delayed for a time, but there would have been no Assam left. Gopinath Bardoloi with his farsightedness and sagacity, revolutionary zeal and heroic leadership rescued Assam and her people from the mischievous conspiracy of foreign rulers. Revered by the people as a true patriot and a disciplined Gandhian, Gopinath Bardoloi was a statesman of high stature. He steered Assam through a very crucial phase of its history and saved Assam becoming a part of Pakistan.

II

Gopinath Bordoloi

Gopinath Bordoloi (6 June 1890 – 5 August 1950) was a politician and Indian independence activist who served as the first Chief Minister of Assam. He was a follower of the Gandhian principle of non-violence as a political tool. Due to his unselfish dedication towards Assam and its people, the then Governor of Assam Jayram Das Doulatram conferred him with the title Lokapriya (loved by all).

Gopinath Bordoloi's political life started when he joined the Indian National Congress as a volunteer in 1921. He actively participated in the fight for independence. He was arrested in 1922 due to active participation in the Non-co-operation movement and was put in jail for a year. When the movement was called off following the Chauri Chaura incident, he went back to practising law. From 1930 to 1933, he kept himself away from all political activity and got involved in various social works after becoming member of Guwahati Municipal Board and Local Board. In addition, he was constantly demanding a separate University and High Court for Assam.

In 1935 Government of India Act was articulated with a view to form British India. Congress decided to participate in the Regional Assembly election in 1936. They won 38 seats and became the party with majority in Assembly, but due to a dubious law meant to reduce the power of Ministers and the Cabinet, they decided to remain as opposition party instead of forming the government. Gopinath Bordoloi was elected as the leader of the opposition party. With the support of other parties apart from Congress, Md. Sadulla formed the Cabinet of Ministers. The Congress party was gaining people's support as the government remained unaware of the basic problems of Assam. The Md. Sadulla Cabinet Ministers resigned in September 1938. The Governor then invited Gopinath Bordoloi to form the government and accordingly they took oath on 21 September 1938.

The reasons of Gopinath Bordoloi becoming Chief Minister of undivided Assam were his political prowess, superb personality, truthfulness and behaviour which attracted not only his colleagues but also people of various communities. Congress got recognition as a powerful political party in Assam by virtue of his ability and intelligence. His contributions as Chief Minister were mainly to stop Land Tax, stop giving lands to migrant Muslims to secure the right of indigenous people etc.

The new government did not last long as World War II began in 1939. Gopinath Bordoloi's Cabinet resigned in 1940 following an appeal by Mohandas K. Gandhi. He was arrested again in December 1940. However, he was released before completing one year in jail due to ill health.

When Quit India movement was launched in August 1942, the Congress party was declared outlawed and all leaders were arrested. In the meantime, Md. Sadulla formed the government with the promise to help British in World War II and indulged again in communal activities. Gopinath Bordoloi was released from jail in 1944 and he straightaway started opposing the government with the help of other leaders. Md.

Sadullah then offered to discuss the matters. An agreement was reached which included immediate release of all political prisoners, removing the ban on procession or meeting, correcting the process of rehabilitation of migrant Muslims, etc.

In July 1945, the British announced their decision to form a new constitution for India after holding the central and regional election. Congress too participated in the election in 1946 and they became the major party in Assembly with 61 seats out of 108. They formed the Government and Gopinath Bordoloi was made Prime Minister unanimously.

The British Government formed the Cabinet Mission of 1946 to discuss the demands for Indian Independence. The members held meetings with the Congress and the Muslim League in Shimla and Delhi. Their plan included grouping of states into 3 categories for selecting the candidates to form the constitutional body with Assam and Bengal in third group. Gopinath Bordoloi sensed the ominous sign for Assam in the plan as the inclusion would mean the local representatives will become minority in comparison to Bengal. That would be devastating for rights of people of Assam.

The Assam Pradesh Congress Committee decided to go against the grouping plan. Gopinath Bordoloi told the Indian National Congress working committee, Cabinet committee and the Viceroy that the representatives of Assam will form the Constitution of Assam themselves and will decide whether to join the group or not among themselves. Subsequently, the Cabinet commission announced that the grouping will be mandatory for every state and they may later withdraw from the group if they want. This further complicated the situation. Bordoloi met the Indian National Congress leaders to discuss it with no result. He then, with the Assam Congress Committee, decided to start mass agitation in Assam. Only after this, the Indian National Congress working committee advised them to pass a unanimous decision in Assembly.

Later, the members of the Assembly suggested a working formula in which ten representatives from Assam would form their own constitution without joining any group and would merge with national committee to form the Indian constitution.

In 1947, Lord Mountbatten took over as new Viceroy. He held separate meetings with the Muslim League, Congress and Mahatma Gandhi. They decided to go for Partition as a permanent solution instead of grouping. India and Pakistan became separate independent countries.

Thus, Gopinath Bordoloi played a major role in securing the future of Assam which would have been included in East Pakistan otherwise.

III

Gurudev Kalicharan Brahma

The great social reformer Gurudev Kalicharan Brahma was born at Kazigaon village in the District of undivided Goalpara on 18th April 1860. Now his birth place is under Kokrajhar district of Bodoland Territorial Region. His father's Name was Kaularam Mech and Mother's was Randini Mech. Kaularam was a timber merchant and one of the rich persons of those days.

From the childhood Kalicharan was a very intelligent, honest and thoughtful. He founded a new religion called "Brahma Dharma" in 1906 and he is reverentially called "Gurudev" or "Guru Brahma" by Bodo people of lower Assam along Brahmaputra river. He also became a great religious preacher of Brahma faith and brought over revolutionary changes in Bodo society by his continuous and sustained programme of reformation.

By the end of the 19th century and the early part of 20th century, the Bodo society was also politically degradation. The young Kalicharan Brahma could perceive the deplorable condition of the Bodos who were bogged down with social practices due to which the commitments despised them and he believed that Bodos are the original inhabitants of Assam. Later Kalicharan Brahma realized that Bodo society would have to be reformed. The Bodos were annoyed by other societies for their bad habits and ill practices. They were addicted to wine, rice bear and bad habits. Later Kalicharan Brahma achieved success in bringing changes among Bodo society in many fields by preaching his religious faith and principles and for which he was known as "Gurudev."

The basic ideology of "Brahma Dharma" preached by Gurudev Kalicharan Brahma is one "God" in the form of "Fire." "Fire" is "Brahma" and "Brahma" gives live to the entire earth and all its begins. "Brahma" is universal and endless. Where there is "Brahma", there can be found "Satya" or "Truth".

IV

Satish Chandra Basumatary

Satish Chandra Basumatary was an Indian Bodo poet, dramatist, social worker and the second president of Bodo Sahitya Sabha. He is a pioneer people of Bibar era, the age of renaissance of Bodo literature. He is credited with helping established Bodo Brahma Dharma. He was also the editor of first Bodo magazine Bibar in 1924. He was honoured Mengnw Rwngwi Jwhwlao title after his death.

He was born on 16 November 1901 at Balukmari village in Dhubri district (present day Kokrajhar district) into a Bodo family. He was the son of Thandaram Basumatary and Khowlou Basumatary. He started schooling from Dhubri High School and later went to Cotton College, Guwahati. He died on 16 November 1974.

V

Rupnath Brahma

Rupnath Brahma was born on 15th June 1902 in a Bodo family at Owabari village near Kokrajhar town. Rupnath Brahma was an active worker of the Bodo Chatra Sanmilan which was established by Gurudev Kalicharan Brahma in the year 1919.

Simon Commission was appointed in November 1927 by the British Conservative government under Stanley Baldwin to report on the working of the Indian constitution established by the Government of India Act of 1919. The commission consisted of seven members - four Conservatives, two Labourites and one Liberal - under the joint chairmanship of the distinguished Liberal lawyer Sir John Simon and Clement Attlee, the future prime minister. Its composition met with a storm of criticism in India because Indians were excluded. The commission was boycotted by the Indian National Congress and most other Indian political parties. It, nevertheless, published a two volume report, mainly the work of Simon.

Regarded as a classic state document, the report proposed provincial autonomy in India but rejected parliamentary responsibility at the centre. It accepted the idea of federalism and sought to retain direct contact between the British crown and the Indian states. Before its publication its conclusions had been outdated by the declaration of October 1929, which stated that dominion status was to be the goal of Indian constitutional development. The coming of the Simon Commission in 1927 provided the necessary springboard for their switchover. The Simon Commission reached Assam in 1928 and remained functional in the state till January 1929. The objective of this Commission was to inquire into the working of the system of Government, the growth of education and development of representative institutions in British India and to report as to whether and to what extent, it was desirable to establish the principle of responsible Government. The Royal Notification served throughout the Indian Domain in March 6, 1928 called for memoranda to be submitted to the Commission. The Boros too submitted memoranda through different organizations of their community. Gurudev Kalicharan Brahma led the delegation team of the Goalpara District Community, while Jadav Khaklari submitted another memorandum as the Secretary of the Assam Kachari Juba Sanmelan, on behalf of the entire Boro community of Assam. The memoranda urged the Government to grant a separate electorate for the Boro-Kachari community, both in the Assembly and local board elections, to provide compulsory free primary education to the students of this community. The memoranda also appealed the Government not to transfer Assam to Bengal province and

recommended for a single chamber ministry for Assam. The memoranda submitted by the Boro-Kachari organizations however did not receive due response from the Government. Intellectuals, who have gone through the original report of the Commission sense foul-play by an Assamese member, who was entrusted with the responsibility of receiving the memoranda from the organizations. However, the memorandum submitted by the Provincial Government redressed Boro grievances to some extent.

He was serious about his education and therefore refused to join the Quit India Movement of 1921 during his college days, for he realized at a very young age that he had to siphon the knowledge acquired, to help his brother Bodos to emancipate. Although he was born in a privileged Timber Merchant's family and was an Advocate (first law graduate from Bodo society) by profession, he quit practising as he did not enjoy the ways and mores of the profession and could not taste success like some of his contemporaries in the then Dhubri Court, who took full advantage of lack of education and simplicity of the poor Bodo people.

He decided to follow the path of Kalicharan Brahma of working towards the development of Bodos and the other Tribal groups as well. Therefore, he came into close contact with him and jointly took up several social welfare activities for the Bodos and other backward communities.

The Government of India Act 1935 sowed the seeds of Political aspirations among Bodos and other backward Tribals in Assam as it provided for the reservation of six seats in the Provincial Assembly for the Plains Tribes. Rupnath Brahma was not only qualified but he wanted to work towards the uplift of the depressed classes. Hence, he was elected as one of the representatives in the 1937 General Election. Later he won from the Sidli Constituency on the ticket of The Tribal League. This election was a historic moment for the Tribal League because as many as five representatives from the Tribal League had been elected to the Provincial Legislature and they could float their concerns and put up the demands of the Tribal people on the floor of the Assembly.

Rupnath Brahma in his speech in the Assam Legislative Assembly Proceedings (ALAP) of 5th August 1937 had raised the issue of preserving the Line System and he cited the example of erstwhile Goalpara. Many Tribal people in Goalpara have been compelled to leave their homes and settle elsewhere. Therefore, he and his colleagues from The Tribal League could gauge the treacherous intention of the Muslim League related to the Line System. Hence the Tribal League backed the Indian National Congress (INC) and played a pertinent role by coming down heavily on the Muslim League and subsequently the government fell on 13th September 1938, which in turn played a decisive factor in the win of INC led by Gopinath Bardoloi on 19th September 1938. Subsequently, Rupnath Brahma was rewarded for his effort and was given the portfolio of the Minister of Forest and Registration as a nominee of the Tribal League. When Rupnath Brahma was the president of All Assam Plains Tribal League he had sent a memorandum to His Excellency the Viceroy stating that the proposed grouping of Assam with Bengal has naturally created a sense of great disapproval and resentment and that the Tribal people of Assam are unanimously against the inclusion of Assam with Bengal.

Rupnath Brahma also lamented, that authorities had sidelined the issue of education of Backward Tribal people of the region. In his Assam Legislative Assembly Proceedings (ALAP) speech on 18th February 1938, he said that he was disappointed with the fact that the government had not earmarked provision for the Plain Tribal people in that year's Budget even though Tribals were the most Backward in the region. He further said, "If there is no definite move from the government for the education of these people, then I think all nation-building projects will be left far behind in Assam". Rupnath Brahma (who had studied in a Bengali medium school) had realized that as a result of the Treaty of Yandaboo, till 1872 Bengali was the medium of instruction and although, Assamese was reintroduced but in many schools of lower Assam, Bengali was still the medium of instruction. Therefore Rupnath Brahma along with Kalicharan Brahma and Sarat Goswami made relentless efforts to introduce Assamese as a medium of instruction in erstwhile Goalpara instead of the prevailing Bengali medium at that time.

Rupnath Brahma had the opportunity to serve the backward and downtrodden tribals when he became a member of the Advisory Committee of the Minority Sub-Committee or Bardoloi sub-committee formed on 27th February 1947. As a member of these committees, he obtained some facilities from the Central Government that would serve the interest of the Tribals. As a member of the Assam Tribal and Excluded Areas Sub-Committee, he rendered yeoman's service to the Sub-Committee. The present Sixth Schedule was added to the Constitution of India on the recommendation of this Sub-Committee.

The Tribal League was formed in 1933 under the leadership of Rupnath Brahma and Rabi Chandra Kachari. In 1937, the Muslim League moved a resolution for the abolition of the Line system. Members of the Tribal League, Rabi Chandra Kachari and Rupnath Brahma opposed the resolution and it was eventually withdrawn. The Tribal League had to fight with the Muslim League under the leadership of Maulavi Saiyid Muhammad Saadulla in Assam Legislative Assembly from 1937 to 1946. Then Tribal League had joined hands with Indian national congress under the leadership of Gopinath Bodoloi after independence.

VI

Jogendra Kumar Basumatary

Jogendra Kumar Basumatary (19 May 1920 - 28 March 2010) was an Indian writer and social worker from Bodo community. He was elected as a president of Bodo Sahitya Sabha held in 1983. He received the first U.N. Brahma Soldier of Humanity Award in 2004.

He was born on 19 May 1920 at Gosaigaon village under Manikpur circle in Goalpara district (present day Kokrajhar district) of Assam. He was the son of Arindra Basumatary and Gilashri Basumatary. He breathed his last on 28 March 2010.

Jogendra Kumar Basumatary was not only a writer and social worker but also a freedom fighter. Police arrested him twice for participating in the freedom struggle. During Quit India Movement, he was arrested and jailed for 6 moths at Guwahati jail.

After independence, he was honoured with Tamrapatra by the Central Goverment and granted him pension in 1973. The State Goverment honoured also him in 1993 by giving him literary pension for his valuable contribution to the Bodo literature. The Upendranath Brahma Trust (UNBT) also honoured him with its first UN Brahma Soldier of Humanity Award for his immense contribution in all fields during 2004.

VII
Conclusion

Finally, Assam became a part of the Indian Union only after a tug-of-war between the Congress and Tribal League versus Muslim League. Mohammad Ali Jinnah made strong claims for the state's inclusion in Pakistan but tenacious opposition from the Congress leadership in the state with Mahatma Gandhi's direct support saved Assam from joining Pakistan. The Assam Congress's determined opposition ensured that the arrangement did not take off. The Cabinet Mission may have sought to preserve the unity of India, but it compromised with the Muslim League on the inclusion of Assam, a Hindu majority province, in Pakistan.

In February 1946, Pethic Lawrence, the then secretary of state for India, circulated a note on the viability of Pakistan. In the note, he mentioned that Assam, due to economic, defence and financial considerations was to form part of East Pakistan. The Assamese were aghast and felt this was a clever British ploy to keep their commercial interests intact. The Cabinet Mission sought to camouflage its real intention by keeping the grouping clause vague and created an impression that they were not serious about exerting pressure on Assam in consonance with the Muslim League's demand.

On May 16, 1946, the Cabinet Mission recommended that Assam and Bengal be tagged together to frame the provisional constitutions for the provinces. The Mission laid stress on provincial autonomy and viewed that every province be constituted on a linguistic and cultural basis. The recommendation came by despite the appearance of Assam Premier Gopinath Bardoloi before the Mission. Bardoloi said, "Assam had always been a separate state with a distinctive identity and must be allowed to remain in India under a provincial status."